DIRT ROADS

AND PLACES THEY TAKE YOU

POETRY AND MEMOIRS

Barbara Jean Ruther

Dirt Roads and Places They Take You

© 2015 Barbara Jean Ruther

Print ISBN: 978-1-68222-329-1

ebook ISBN: 978-1-68222-330-7

As you read my poetry,
think gentle of me,
for you will have seen my soul….

BJR

CONTENTS

OFF THE DIRT ROADS —TO PLACES IN MY HEART

THE END OF THE ROAD —NOT EVEN A STOP SIGN

FOR KATHRYN, MOLLY AND JESSICA —
on their own roads

THE ROAD TO MEMORIES —
A GOOD PLACE TO WALK

DIRT ROADS

A relaxed mailbox out by the ditch
might have a name scrawled on it.
Otherwise, they say,
"Take the second dirt road past the arroyo."
Weeds spill from clumps of dry soil,
tired fences of discarded vigas
are held together with reused barbed wire,
keeping the heifers at home.

Adobe haciendas grow from the earth
with modest windows, a little uneven
and screen doors that don't quite close.
There's a gathering of rusty garbage cans,
a couple peculiar dogs lying in the shade,
monstrous and shaggy cottonwoods
decorated with clusters of stubborn hollyhocks,
no one thinks about watering.

Occasional pickup trucks stir the dust,
brown clouds glisten in the sun,
announce a visitor.
They come to spend evenings
on a rickety porch swing,
watch the sky change hues, drink iced tea.
There's a peacefulness and calm
like the breathing of a sleeping baby.

Placed in *Writer's digest* Annual Poetry Contest
Published on *New Mexico Magazine* Webpage
Published in *Jean's Journal* Poetry Magazine

A PLACE OF MEMORIES

I'll go back to Sulphur Springs.
They will still be there —
Papa, laced in his high-top shoes,
gathering crispy-dry wood.
Mama, in her Irish temper,
bossing out job orders,
the pitched Army tent, cots piled
with surplus-store blankets,
the smell of cedar, and coffee —
a handful of grounds boiled in water,
bacon sizzling in an iron skillet
supported by rocks over a campfire.

I'll go back to Sulphur Springs,
drink the earth's lemon-water,
lie in the worn wooden tub filled
with smelly yellow liquid.
"Good for achy bones," Papa said.
Come sit with me on the wood plank
at the edge of the rotten-egg foot bath.
Reach under the seat and get a handful
of caked sulphur mud
to smear on our arms and faces.
"It will make us beautiful," Mama promised.
We will laugh at each other's masks.

→

I'll go back to Sulphur Springs,
sit cross-legged
on the brown pine-needled ground,
share buttered tortilla with chipmunks.
This time I won't be afraid
of hoots and crackles in the night.
I'll hook that wriggly worm on the barb
and feed him to freckled trout.
Come, let our feet go numb
in the icy creek where Uncle Frank
anchored watermelons to keep them cold.

Sulphur Springs — A place to make memories

Published in *The New Mexican* Newspaper - Third place annual writing contest

SAVING SNOWFLAKES IN MY POCKET

Some Memories are like butterflies,
too fragile to be held in the palm of your hand,
elusive as wings on a breeze,
the sight lingering long after they are gone.

Some Memories are like delicate roses,
doomed to perish from the day they are gathered,
causing tears and dried petals to fall
and mingle on the floor of a sad soul.

Some Memories are like seashells,
scattered across the sands of life,
waiting to be collected and saved in a jar,
placed on a shelf for a rainy day of remembering.

Some Memories are like apple seeds.
Planted in a grounded heart, they sprout tenderly
and grow into a blossomed tree of life,
bearing fruit to reward the laborer.

Some Memories are like snowflakes.
No matter how hard you try to save them,
they melt away and leave a stain
in an empty pocket
and in an empty heart.

Published in the novel *Saving Snowflakes in My Pocket*

JEANNIE'S FRECKLES

Those little brown spots
polka-dotted her nose —
burrs in the sweet clover of pretty
in the world of a ten year old.
Her bottom lip stuck out
in a swollen bud pout
when we called her freckles "cute."

She tried to squeeze them off
between two fingernails like pimples,
soap-scrubbed fragile cheeks to red-raw,
rubbed at the flecks with lemon juice. . . .
until a fifth-grade boy said,
"Where'd you get those freckles?"
Then they decorated her smile.

Published in *Thirteen* Poetry Magazine

HER ELEVENTH CHILD

Her foreign-born husband
called her Mama.
As did ten mischievous children,
the biscuits-and-gravy-fed boarders,
Indians from the nearby Pueblo
and mixed-race people in the dreary town.
Then, all the grandchildren called her Mama,
even me, the granddaughter she raised.
"My eleventh child," she said.

Not everyone called her husband Papa.
A mountainous man with leathery hands,
his presence allowed no laughing.
A tough bargainer, he traded cattle
with the Indians and haggled in their language.
He sold fresh-butchered calves
to the locals and spoke Spanish.
At home he imposed his strict discipline
on the children and shouted in Arabic.
At night, he whispered to Mama in English,
a gentle way no one else knew in him.

Mama's index memory spun back — scabbed fingers
from picking cotton in a desolate Texas town,
meeting a dark stranger at scrappy fourteen,
becoming his buckboard bride and
settling down in dusty Domingo, New Mexico.
Mama sat in her calico-cushioned rocker,
I snuggled by her used-up breasts
to hear stories I already knew.

→

We explored an exhausted satchel —
yellowed family pictures, birth records,
baptismal certificates, scraps of letters.
With those treasures, we relived her life.

Mama left the satchel and its bounty for me.
They bring back the memories and make me cry.
Without my old companion,
the pictures have no words.

Published in *Poetic Justice* Poetry Magazine

CHILDREN OF MY HEART

They are the scrappy, the scrawny, the scared
with bruised bodies and souls.
Fear has dulled their eyes,
caused them to hide inside themselves,
lost in a tangle of roars and rage.
I want to give them cushioned safety,
a place to laugh out loud,
to get tickles in their tummy
down the slide and up the swing of being.

I am the reader of nursery rhymes,
the hugger, the hip carrier,
the soft talker, the smiler,
the giver of apple juice and Band-Aids.
I try to bury the memory of hurt,
but like the buried red ant,
it crawls back up to the top
and stings their smile.

Published in the novel *Saving Snowflakes in My Pocket*

HAVING RUN THE CREEK

Aunt Nettie stared into space
like those glass-eyed dolls.
After 45 years, morning coffee alone,
wrapped in his red-flannel
dear-hunting shirt.

She had married the curly haired cowboy
ten days after they met, carried along
like Spring thaw running the creek.
He left bride and horse to soldier —
off to Normandy.

He wouldn't eat lunch at the Senior Center.
"I'm only seventy-two,
those people are old."
Uncle Brown bore the weight of cancer
like another duty in war.

Veterans folded the coffin flag yesterday.
He had picked the spot, under a pine.
"A ten-point buck I know might visit me,
snack on the bark of that spruce.
We'll talk over the times I missed him."

Published in *The Cathartic*   Published in *Pegasus*

ROCKY MOUNTAIN BRIDE

Boot-heel marks decorate
a bare-floor bar in a
Rocky Mountain mining town.
The eyes of a young bride,
missing from the senior prom,
watch sloshy movements at the pool table —
her beer-faced groom in new Levi's.

I observe the moppet face,
propped on disappointed hands,
a tear threatening to appear,
reflected in the leaded-glass windows.
It's her wedding night,
sitting on a barstool
in a J.C. Penny's puffed-sleeve dress.

My own daughter's face
keeps replacing hers.
I remove a gold chain
and clasp it around her wrist.
"Your wedding gift!"
It's skimpy as the band on her finger,
but her cheeks blush a glow
and thaw her smile.

Published in *Up Against The Wall, Mother*

REMEMBERING AUNT EMMA

I dragged the footstool to sit at your feet,
be mesmerized by stories of your youth.
Your Grandma taught you to sew
on her old Singer treadle machine.
You hemmed chicken-feed sacks
to make flowered dishtowels.
Then I watched you sew seams and hems
on silks and linens
with your sleek new Singer.
You said, "We can't walk along the river today,
must let out this jacket for the banker's wife
who gained ten pounds."
We snickered,
"Must shorten this skirt for the short preacher's wife."
I didn't know that was the money to buy our groceries.
Seldom, we got a note and little cash.
You never said, "About time!" or "Only this?"
You always said, "Your sweet Mother remembered us."
But, Aunt Emma, you were my sweet Mother.
You soothed my fevered head,
kissed my scraped knee, mended my hurt feelings,
read to me of 'happily ever after'
and sent me on my way,
your loving smile ingrained on my mind.

But, you had to leave, too tired to stay, I think.
Who's going to patch my broken heart?

Published in the novel *Saving Snowflakes in My Pocket*

THE BREAD MAKER

Tub-sized bowl, flour, lard, baking soda,
but how much of each?
"Just 'til it feels right."
Aunt Shadie knows the feel.
She kneads and gives her blessing,
bringing the dough to life.

Chummy charcoal eyes in cave openings
invite me in to gossip.
I exaggerate, to make her smile.
"¿Son meñtires?" (Are those lies?) She grins,
repeating the old adage from Peña Blanca,
a frowning New Mexican town.

Loaves, biscuits, tortillas —
the first batch gone before cool
to unwashed hands
of her five giggly children.
She is happy with the empty pan,
out-the-door thanks.

Aunt Shadie is sick —
who's going to make the bread
and smile at my lies?

Published in *American Poetry Anthology*   Published in *Jean's Journal* Poetry Magazine

MILLIONS OF CELLS OF REBELLION

There is no music-noise surrounding his room,
and stillness draws me like a magnet.
I sit at his desk to absorb leftover presence
like a shadowed plant reaching for the window.
My heart hangs heavy — out loud I said,
"I'll be glad when you're out of this house."
Could he have been that bad?
He was millions of cells of rebellion,
shook the pedestal to topple authority.
Did I run the ship too tight, provoke the mutiny?
To give a curfew was to hope the sun wouldn't set.
Asking him to study was to calm stormy seas.

I want him back as the little boy —
the one who found me crying
and the duckling body became a soldier's,
ready for battle if I named the enemy,
the boy who brought tulips
from our neighbor's yard,
wrote notes of love on my grocery list,
ran home to repeat the new Knock Knock joke
so I would marvel at his cleverness.
We captured crickets in baby food jars
and spoke with our eyes
when we saw a deer in the forest preserve.

→

Did I draw his map with paths too narrow?
He chose roads that said, One Way - Do Not Enter
and littered the route with loud music and drugs.
He packed his clothes, laughed off to college.
My mother-wise advice and his sandbox
rotted and rusted and joined the earth.

His sterile room is my womb —
empty again.

Published in *Up Against The Wall, Mother*

A LETTER NOT SENT

Dear Jessie Sue,

It's a long way from fifth grade,
El Rancho School, Albuquerque,
to married, mother of twins, Australia.
You left the Jessie and me
on Fourth Street,
took just the Sue.
Do you ever think of me,
your Best-Friend-Forever?

You were a Norman Rockwell girl,
freckles and knobby knees,
ears poking out in front of pigtails.
I had gotten my first camera,
every picture was of you, and you and me —
rolled up jeans, our Dads' shirts hanging,
two bean poles in Woolworth bathing suits,
murky from the irrigation ditch.

Wait! Stop! Let me read this letter.
What does it say?
I'm propped up with Ralph Lauren pillows,
putting down in black and white,
as they say, that I actually swam
in an irrigation ditch!
Well, no one will believe it, of course.
Me? — with a hair style and pedicured pink toes?

→

Perhaps, I won't write this letter, Jessie Sue.
No one will know when we were eleven —
you and I went with Alton and Jimmy
down the dirt road to a vacant lot,
a thick patch of elm trees.
"Just a picnic," we said
and kissed all afternoon
intermingled with grape Kool-Aid and giggles.

Later, we were horrified —
our tongues were purple!
We kissed each other
to see if we had done it right,
if our kisses tasted purple-grape.
Does Kool-Aid in Australia remind you of me?
If we could spend a day together
I would even call you Sue.

You would know at once
my gray hair is dyed blond
and support pantyhose hold in my stomach.
You would hear unspoken apologies —
sorry I never told you
your kiss tasted purple.
Sorry, I never said I was happy
you found a new Best-Friend-Forever.

MIDDLECHILD

You were born mid-row of the family garden,
crowded by a spreading-ivy brother
who covered all ground to the border,
left no showing-off space for you.

Then, that posy of a sister, pink and peppy,
soaked up all the sunny smiles.
Yet shaded and squeezed, you bloomed,
sturdy and quiet as a lily.

Your style was not resentment.
You bragged about your brother skiing,
never complained when your sister
returned your blouse all smudgy.

I thought, perhaps you buried
some anger towards me.
Did I put the spotlight on your brother?
Over coddle your sister?

You nestled your hand in mine.
We mother-daughter talked
about the riddle of boys,
the honeycomb of relationships.

Published in *Poets at Work*

THE FLIGHT ATTENDANT

She rises with the sun,
paints her face like an artist,
lacquers each hair in place.
Ralph Lauren Uniform — Check
Pin-up legs, stiletto heels.
A dash in the Camaro to Kennedy.
Vanity license — FLYWHME.

New York to Chicago —
"Does this airline serve
something besides chicken?"
"Madam, Maxim's serves steaks,
we give airplane rides."
"This blanket is dirty!"
"Sorry, I'm not on laundry duty."

Chicago to Denver —
"Model-handsome in 12C looking."
"Blue socks with brown shoes,
you can have him."
"Call light at row 6A."
"The Scotch drinker,
tell him this is Portland."

Denver to Los Angeles —
Tired strands of hair
hanging over smudged mascara,
coffee stained skirt and hose with runs.
"Lose something under the seat?"
"I'm looking for the glamour
in this glamorous job!"

For the TWA girls that flew coast to coast

AUNT FLORENCIE'S FAMOUS FUDGE

Your life seems simple
as a one-room schoolhouse,
restrained as nun-ruled children.
We smile at a disarray of curly hair,
throw-on-and-go elastic-waist pants
and a Sears much-washed shirt.
Your groceries include jellybeans
to stuff in back pockets
of young neighbors' jeans.

You talk gruff as Scrooge —
"Don't expect presents or
a Christmas tree at my house this year."
We see your Chevy coming down the road,
a big Blue Spruce sticking from the trunk
like a curious child peeking 'round a door.
Out of the closet come sheltered decorations,
collected through years,
kept like cherished friends.

Days are spent making
batches of our Christmas presents.
Dozens of nieces and nephews
stop by to pick from
assorted recycled boxes and tins,
all tied with uneven bows,
each filled with your secret recipe.
Beneath your turtle-shell you blush
as we chant, "Three cheers for
Aunt Florencie's Famous Fudge."

Published in *Kaleidoscope: Women at Work*

THE POSITIVE AMONG NEGATIVES

Born the last of ten children
to an elderly mother at menopause,
life and school were challenges, an uphill climb,
but with summer school sessions
you proudly graduated High School at age twenty.

You lived a life of negatives —
No prom date to bring a carnation corsage,
No fancy dresses with ruffled skirts,
No cruises to Hawaiian Islands,
No dinners at valet restaurants about which to brag,
No courting suitors with promises,
No husband and child to enclose in your Christmas card,
No kinds words of thanks from nine siblings
for years you tended the mother of all.

You often sank into loneliness, but kept afloat by visiting
any family member who would accept you, but so few.
You longed for hugs, but were uncomfortable returning them.
Your heart overflowed with love you were not quite sure
how to share. Oh how you tried.
You sent checks from your meager income — to graduates,
brides and grooms, anyone sending an announcement.
You yearned for companionship, bribed with your home-cooking,
just to have someone sit at your table.

→

Too late we realized we should have been proud of you,
proud of the way you lived alone for forty-two years,
proud for supporting yourself with your limited ability,
proud you made us guiltless for not helping you,
proud you drove yourself to a lifetime of doctor's appointments,
until you lost your way.
The end of life in sight, a virgin into your wheelchair,
breasts stolen by cancer,
we asked ourselves, "Were you happy in your life?"

The answer was in your smile when we walked in your door

For Aunt Florencie

THE RAIN DANCE

Hidden from prying highways,
tucked between rock-strewn mesas,
growing from the sun-baked earth,
the hand-labored adobe pueblo.
I studied the traditions of the native ceremonies,
brought my child to sit on crusted ground
and be hypnotized by ancient rituals.

Young Indian men go away to college,
trade moccasins for work-boots or Gucci loafers,
all return home to dance in The Fiesta,
a ceremonial plea for rain on the corn crop.
Hair cut short for better fitting in,
but enough left to attach the parrot feathers,
symbols of heavenly creatures.

The day begins the same as one hundred years ago,
visit the whitewashed adobe church,
acknowledge the missionaries' God.
Costumed as ancestors were in assigned places,
a male with bare, muscular chest leads the dancers.
Leathered at his throat, the single large shell,
symbol of sacred water.

→

Toddlers alongside their mothers,
knowing their true parents are Sun and Earth.
Only women dance barefoot to have contact
with Mother Earth, receive her fertility.
Shining in the sun is straight, hip-length hair,
rough and coarse as the mesa's black lava rock.
All adorned with turquoise, the sky-colored sacred stone.

The drum's thunder-beat vibrates through bodies,
chanting by a chorus of elders,
an inherited honor.
Words recited are so sacred
not one syllable dare be changed,
meaning lost in antiquity,
but chanted without question.

I intrude on my child's trance,
"We must leave soon, the rain will begin."
Young doubting eyes search the aqua sky –
no clouds.
Feet stamp in rhythmic unison, the flag carrier
swoops a prayer-pole over dancer's heads
to sweep up prayers, sending them heavenward.

As we leave the plaza's dry heat,
drums stop suddenly,
the silence is loud,
prayers for rain have finished.
Driving home, I watch my child's quiet face.
He stares straight ahead at the windshield wipers
parting the pouring rain.

Published in the novel *Saving Snowflakes in My Pocket*   Published in *Sing Heavenly Muse*

WILD - IN - THE - WIND

Where did it come from, that standing in awe
admiration of horses? Not from her mother
who didn't even like pony rides
at friend's age-six birthday parties.
Not from her mother's mother who
had watched girlfriend's do barrel races
at local rodeos, but kept the weathered-board
fence between her and the horses.
The pictures were thumb-tacked
to her wall, taped to her mirror —
horses standing on rear hooves,
horses grazing in carpet meadows,
horses prancing in parade.
Hesitantly I bought riding lessons.
She combed the assigned horse,
called her Sally, praised her trot.
We took pictures, horse and child
cheek to cheek, each week a hug goodbye.
I took her to the mountains of New Mexico
to stare at the wild-in-the-wind mustangs.
Driving around sage and cedar scrub,
lost to buildings and parking meters,
twenty shaggy-maned horses.
Wide-eyed, she got out of the Jeep,
hands behind her, eyes lowered as she
had been taught, and took two steps closer.

→

The stallion — muscular chest, head held high,
eyes attentive, nostrils flaring,
left the group and walked toward her.
My heart double-timed. He stopped.
What was he thinking, this powerful animal,
observing this child? Was she a threat?
She was looking at a new foal, nestled
against its mother's belly.
Perhaps he understood, a child watching a child.
He turned and walked slowly to the mare.
She had been dismissed, so she returned
to the Jeep, watched until we bumped
over the hills, out of sight.

For Kathryn

OUR WALKS ALONG THE DITCH

The memory of her
fills my mind
like dreams through sleep,
sloshes inside my soul
like the surf rolling ashore.

She kneaded the dough
for our sustenance,
but my life came from her love,
a mixture she also molded,
shaped, flavored, crusted.

Today, I would tell her
my body misses the doughy hugs,
our walks along the ditch
to cut wild asparagus,
emptying dirt from our shoes,
together.

For Aunt Shadie

MOTHERING

It could have been years since I had seen her and then, like that unexpected summer shower, she would just appear. As a child, I was never quite sure if she truly existed or if her appearances were something mysterious, like a rainbow. This strange relationship didn't only occur during my childhood, but throughout my life.

One evening, dinner dishes being sloshed in the dishwasher, the two- and four-year-olds asleep under mounds of teddy bears, deeply engrossed with my old flame, Cary Grant, the ringing of the telephone jolted me back to reality. I listened as a Southern-sweet voice said, "Hello, Barbara Jean, this is your Mommy."

Some of my Aunts still called me by this double-name, affectionately left over from their protective caring of a mother-orphaned child. I knew my mother referred to herself as my "Mommy," it was signed on the occasional birthday card. But at this stage in my life — married, ensconced in a Chicago suburb, two children, six months pregnant and well into my thirties, it was upsetting, confusing, like getting caught in a revolving door, to be expected to think of her as my "Mommy." Especially since my own children called me "Mom." One time my husband had made the mistake of saying to them, "Take these newspapers to your Mom." They came running to me with the folded paper and their new word, "Mom," "Mom," "Mom." That was the end of "Mommy."

Finally, maturity stepped in, I responded like an adult. She was "passing through Chicago tomorrow with a three-hour layover" and could I bring the children to the airport for a short visit?

Please God, let me have no animosity for the years of no phone calls, no valentines, no congratulations at graduations or marriage or births. Let me think of the years of comforting hugs and mending kisses from a grandmother and eight aunts who curled my wispy blond hair into ringlets around their fingers, bought the drink-and-wet dolls for me to learn about mothering. They taught me to sew, hem dish towels from chicken-feed sacks, fashion my own clothes and how to make ice cream in an old wooden bucket with a crank.

"Yes," I answered, "I would be happy to bring the children to the airport to meet you."

The surprise phone call played on my mind like an old song that keeps coming up, and brought memories of my Dad, handsome in his white Stetson. He had not married again for eight years after she left. Was he waiting for her to come back?

The next day, driving to O'Hare airport, I tried to explain in Dr. Seuss words, "We are going to visit your other grandmother. Nana is Daddy's mother and this is my mother."

"What's her name?" Came the question from the four-year-old in the car-seat. Leave it to a child to find the last page, I thought.

"Her name is Gram."

A child clamped to each hand, I silently panicked — would I recognize her? How long since I had seen her? Twelve years? Well, I consoled myself, she may not recognize me. But then, how many blondish, thirty-something women with two little kids and a scared expression could there be?

I saw her! I knew at first glance and my heart began the quick-beat of the runner crossing the finish line. It wasn't a happy-to-see-her feeling, rather the same feeling when I looked months for a special dress to wear at my husband's office party and suddenly The Dress called from a rack. The worried-over dress was looking at me, the anxiousness was over, I had paid the bill. Okay, now what to say to someone I didn't know.

She had several hours before her connection. I offered to take her home for lunch, promising to get her back in time for the next flight. I wondered, had she ever made lunch for me? How old was I when she left Dad and me? The family, all from Dad's side, never talked about her in my presence. I heard no criticism, no faultfinding, no judging, not even information about her life before she met my Dad. Was 'no information' their way of sheltering me? From cousins, I got bits of gossip they had gleaned from their parents — she had married a cowboy, but didn't like horses, said horses smelled and might bite. Then one day, some real news! When the baby was only a few months old, she filed for divorce. The judge awarded the parents alternating six-month periods. The repeated story continued — one week, two weeks? into the mother's custody time, the dad away to Nevada to sell horses, a nun called the baby's grandmother. At the adoption agency where she was now assigned, someone had dropped off a child who had the family name the nun recognized. Sister Maria Magdalena had taught several children with the same name many years earlier in the one-room schoolhouse in dusty Peña Blanca, New Mexico. The baby's grandmother had raised ten children in that rural town, and five others were buried in the cemetery of handmade wooden crosses, next to the weary adobe church. Survival was for the fittest who had harsh determination.

"Yes," the grandmother had replied. "She is my baby, I will bring her home." Just like the box of kittens left on her doorstep that she quietly slipped fresh milk to, the baby became hers, her eleventh child. To all eleven children she was Mama. Mama told me to "never put the cart before the horse, don't count your chickens before they're hatched" and threatened to wash my mouth out with soap. Yet the older children took the blame and punishment, while I got a patient smile of the Mother-hen who scooped the errant chick under her wing. When I left home to explore New York City, my room, with petticoats gushing from the closet, and pink ruffled organdy curtains, remained unoccupied and untouched. I went home often to visit my Mama.

At O'Hare airport, I stared at the woman smiling towards me. She was old-movie-star beautiful — a Jane Russell, an Ava Gardner. She was wearing a pale-blue suit that seemed the same color as her eyes, a gold ribbon-shaped brooch decorated with dark blue stones on her lapel, a navy scarf tucked around her neck, dyed red hair loosely pulled back into a French Twist. She looked earthy enough to drink beer and laugh loud, yet so glamorous everyone who passed, slowed, glanced. She invited looks, not with a high ignoring chin, but friendly, as if she may say, "Y'all come on over for some Southern fried chicken now."

I felt self-consciously fat instead of proud and pregnant. I was dowdy, homey, suburban, with too little makeup and a nervous smile. A quick thought pulsed through my brain — no more chocolate chip cookies, more walking-exercise and get out the cologne. The children were tugging on my loose maternity blouse, yelling, pointing at the popcorn wagon.

She hugged them, picked up the two-year-old, bought them popcorn, gave me a quick kiss on the cheek like she had seen me yesterday. "Nice to see you," I managed to say, just above a whisper, as if she was an old friend.

Driving home, the children's keen sense let them know I probably would not scold if they had a popcorn throwing contest. By the time we turned into the driveway the back of the SUV looked like it had gone through a snowstorm.

Our guest sat at the breakfast-room table with the awed children, while I put together a salmon salad, thinking it was quick to make, but sophisticated. I placed the lettuce just so, heaped the salad on top, big ripe strawberries on the side — pink, red and green, straight from Ladies Home Journal. Proud of myself, I talked in short, partial sentences, concentrating on two important jobs at one time — preparing an elegant-looking plate and sounding impressively intelligent. "Would you like raspberry iced tea or Perrier?" Ah, so worldly!

No Answer!

If this was a friend sitting in my kitchen waiting for lunch and she didn't hear my question, I would say, "Joyce?" or "Susan?" to bring her back to the kitchen in case she had wondered off in thought. But I didn't have a name for this person, that is, I had never called her by a name. I repeated the question. She ignored me and continued her one-way conversation with the children which included, "Sugah Babies, Swee' Thangs, Honay Bees." They knelt on the cushioned chairs leaning towards her, focusing intently on sky-blue eyes with mascara-laden lashes. She held their attention like Big Bird never could.

Anxiety crept through me and settled in my fingers. The ice cubes missed the glasses, slid across the granite countertop and scattered on the tile floor, making little puddles that I wanted to sink into. I knew she was waiting for the name attached to the question.

My mind flashed back to her seldom visits. She had come to our house three times during my High School days. Mama sat stiff and straight in her over-stuffed chair. The purple crocheted lap blanket folded to the side, no appearance of being a comfortable, hospitable host. Her lips tight, gaze fixed on the other woman, she sent a message of aversion with her crossed-arms attitude. Later in my life, we had met two more times when she had contacted me after I left home. No, I had never called her a name. Now, should I call her by her first name? It seemed so disrespectful. Oh, Mama, you ingrained that respect-thing on my brain.

I had never said the word, "Mother." I opened my mouth, but it wouldn't come out. It doesn't slide out of your mouth like a lollipop.

"Mother" or "Mama" are words that have permeated the body, soaked in by the cleverness of putting plastic bags on my feet so those difficult boots slipped right on. Or the grilled cheese sandwich for me when everyone else had Uncle Albert's fresh fried trout. ("Mama, I can't eat him, I watched that fish swimming in the creek") Or the unspoken love when she kept hugging and I stopped that told me she didn't want to let me go.

I poured two glasses of iced tea and put one in front of her.

"So, how's your lunch, Gram?"

THE ROAD TO LOVE —
AND SUCH PLACES

THE WHISPERER

I am the sunshine, reflecting
sapphires from your eyes,
the fringed shawl, wool gloves,
an umbrella above your head.

I am the soaring hawk
watching your every move,
the warbler singing his song for you,
the child walking in your footsteps.

I am the honey in your tea,
your macaroni and cheese,
the salt for your popcorn,
a glass of ruby-red wine.

I am the pulsing heartbeat,
the blood in your veins.
I am the man whispering
of love and promise.

From the novel *The Strawberry Field*

THROUGH THE SEASONS OF OUR LIFE
(The Bride's Promise)

Your touch is warm Spring on my shoulders,
causes me to blossom like new velvety irises.
I am the May Day Girl
with bridal wreath in my hair,
laughing a dance for you.
The smile in your eyes reflects a heart's promise
of continuous love —
your soul's declaration of trust.

I will join you into the commitment of Summer rain
for nourishment and growth of family.
From the fresh-washed garden
I will pick a deep red rose,
the color will remind us of our blood
flowing through our children.
Storm clouds will not dim the brightness
of our caring nor our protection of each other.

As trees take their rest, slough off Autumn colors
and it bares your senses,
I will lift your spirits with my game,
like the cool swirling wind plays with the leaves.
The warmth of our bodies pressed together
give us strength to fortify
against the thunder of hurt
and lightning strikes of harm.

→

When youth leaves us to sing her song
among swaying skirts and prancing feet
and our hair turns silver as Winter snow fields,
let us walk side by side down that new path
like the Gray Wolves who mate for life.
Our candle of love will burn bright
in the window of fate
and we will be grateful for memories.

There will be another Spring,
new-growth on the pine trees,
girls with bridal-wreath in their hair,
cherry branches full of fresh buds
that will blossom like young laughter,
as the blood of our children
flows through their children
and the seasons of life pass by us.

From the novel *The Strawberry Field*   Published in the novel
Saving Snowflakes in My Pocket

THE MYSTERY OF LOVE

Gather life into a box of puzzle pieces,
the fragments of our memoir.
Turn the contents upside down —
the accumulation of existence.
Within the pile, used-up pictures
to be matched and locked together,
forming our story.
The mystery of love is a jigsaw puzzle.
The whole scene appears
as the pieces are fitted together.

Published in the novel *Saving Snowflakes in My Pocket*

DISLOYALTY

Your love-whispers
collect into a boomerang,
circle 'round me
and return to pierce
your unfaithful heart.

Published in *Arizona Quarterly*   Published in *Night Roses*
Published in *Thirteen Poetry Magazine*

THE SOUND OF LOVE

The young couple's shoulders slumped
and sank beneath the weighty news.
Their newborn boy with aquamarine eyes
would never walk, never talk,
never draw pictures on the living-room wall.
We looked through a translucent complexion
that revealed the ravaged,
nipped-in-the-bud brain.

Justin's Aunts and Uncles
nested the new family into their home,
where the new mother had married
and left only a year before.
Through the nights he cried,
all took turns at constant cuddling,
until the birdling body adjusted to living.

The months baby-talked away
as almost a spoonful went down,
a forehead kiss
when hardly any milk came back.

Now they kneel beside the wheel-chaired child,
his head hanging limp,
as they receive their reward,
a sound,
the sound of love.

DANGER - THIN ICE

He murmured loyal-love promises,
fragile as the lake's newly formed ice,
then tested her belief
with lie-filled boots
and sunk in cold waters of deceit.

Published in *Poets at Work*

LOVE NOTE

Here is my heart,
I give it to you.
It doesn't want to stay
with me, just keeps
watching for you.
No good for me anymore,
your name scrawled all over.
Keep it in your pocket,
feel the purr like a warm kitten.

From the novel *The Strawberry Field*

HEADED WEST

You slammed the door
on dark cloudy skies
as words hailed
heavy on my shoulders.

You left footprints
frozen in the snow.
My tears like icicles
snapped with goodbye
as I watched you head
for fiery sunsets.

BROKEN, SHATTERED, SNAPPED

That sweet singing wren
flew into the plate glass window,
a broken neck among feathers,
laying like a dishrag on the patio.

The pressed-glass candy dish,
handed down from my grandmother,
fell to the cold, hard tile,
shattered into a million fragments.

Those winter ice-storms
came blowing off the lake,
coated each bare abandoned branch.
They snapped like potato chips.

Now you understand
about my heart.

MOUNTAIN-MAN

The memory of his face appeared —
unruly hair, blowing wild with the wind,
the color a field of ripe wheat,
a smile so honeyed it made me cry.
In the pockets of his windbreaker
he brought tiny strawberries
that grew ripe-red on their own
in the mountain wilderness.
From a secret valley filled
with untamed daisies,
he picked a bouquet,
presented them in a pickle jar.
Perhaps it was all a dream!

Published in the novel *Saving Snowflakes in My Pockets*

ALL ABOARD

He hung out the window
like a Raggedy-Andy,
stretching down to tousle good-bye
some Raggedy-Ann red hair.

Published in *Poets at Work*

JUST ONE TIME

Let me win the game,
raise my arms in the air victorious,
get sprinkled with confetti.

Tell everyone to watch me strut,
twirling a baton in my gold-braided
vest as I lead the parade.

Just one smiling time
announce me the winner,
award the loving cup to me.

Choose me for the Ball,
dressed in swirling pink chiffon
dance me past midnight.

Stand tiptoe on the mountain top,
reach the luminous sky,
collect stars to decorate my hair.

Put me center-stage,
switch bright the spotlight,
listen to my song.

Hang my picture on your wall,
point it out to the crowd,
throw a kiss when you pass.

Put my name in your poem,
spell it with hearts
and just once, love only me.

OFF THE DIRT ROADS —
TO PLACES IN MY HEART

THE COLLECTOR

I walk the same mesa where
Indian braves galloped paint-ponies,
under an infinite sky
colored like the turquoise veins
hidden inside the textured mountains.
Ghosts hover above adobe ruins,
whispering their ancient secrets
of ancestors who lived in cliff dwellings,
where stews cooked in coiled-clay pots
in hornos made of mud bricks.

My breath mingles with the same wind
that scattered campfire ashes
of silent hunters who
aimed arrows at antlered deer.
I step barefoot into the icy creek
where pueblo girls washed midnight hair,
dark and coarse as the lava rock.
Lost history surrounds me
like the hand-woven sheep's-wool blankets
that encircled their shoulders.

I collect bits of Indian lives
and hoard them in my pocket —
time-polished stone arrowheads
whetted by adept hands,
shards of painted pots
that once held sacred water
balanced on steady heads.

→

In my arms I carry pieces of drowned wood
coughed up by the Rio Grande — perhaps
the frame for animal skins, to form tepees.

Then, I close my eyes
and scatter my treasures across dry ground,
knowing they must return to their natural place —

Mother Earth

CAMOUFLAGE

So early the stars
have barely disappeared,
the sun almost peeking
over the mountain.
Wild bunnies with
instilled sense of danger,
creep across the dull thirsty earth,
perhaps to find new growth
at the bottom of a brittle
clump of field grass.

The dry bushes,
the brown soil,
the new bunnies,
all in camouflage, no contrast.
Only the twitching of small noses,
divulge the disguise.

Hiding in wait,
patient as a sniper,
keen eyes like a scope,
small fluffs revealed.
Quick as a shot —

The Coyote

IN SEARCH OF GOLD

Coronado — Conquistador,
rigid with nobility,
helmeted, sworded, armored.
Did you think you had found
the sought-gold?

The Autumn cottonwoods
along the Rio Grande
sprouted millions of gold coins,
winked an invitation,
enticement.

The evening sun welcomed,
allured with a glowing pot,
influenced the blushing clouds,
lustrous with wealth,
a gilded temptation.

Coronado — Conquistador,
you reflected on victory-thoughts.
The gold could not be taken,
so you stayed
to bask in the hue.

LA GITANA TELLS HER LIFE

Flamenco dancer,
rhythmic clapping, a rustle of ruffles,
ballerina arms framing a bud-face,
pulled tight, slick, lustrous hair,
La Gitana strikes her pose.
Stiletto-like crimson nails click castanets,
her quick-pulse music.

A sudden staccato of stomping
loosens her severe hair knot
and Spanish combs fly.
A midnight mane tumbles
from head to slim, girded waist.
Her mother's fringed shawl
slithers from bare shoulders.

Ebony eyes glint with a scowl.
The Gypsy fire-strut shows us
that her ancestors
were caved in Granada,
in the shadow of carved marble,
outside the fountained Alhambra.

Her Andalusian chin lifts high.
With her dance
La Gitana tells her life.

(La Gitana - The Gypsy) Published in *Kaleidoscope: Women at Work*

THE QUIET AUTUMN OF MY LIFE

I remember when the future
seemed distant as the mountains.
Now, I stand atop those hills,
search the past as it sways in the wind
like the shedding willows,
a scurry of leaves
in October's running.

Memories haunt me
as ghosts from my childhood
flicker from The Old House,
the open porch where I performed
as ballerina and cowgirl-singer,
the front steps of Cinderella's palace
where I blushed, a first kiss.

Now a realty beehive with computer-buzz,
the yawning fireplace-cum-bookniche
must wonder whatever happened
to the gangly blond kid
who stood on the hearth each night,
warming bare feet in her flannel nightie
before running to cold sheets.

It is quiet autumn now.
With a wink and a smile,
prancing youth tip-toed away yesterday.
She whispered as she passed,
"Listen gently to bygone verses
of the pealing chimes of life-before,
and just let clouds wander by."

Published in *Yesterdays*   Published in *Kaleidoscope: Women at Work*

TOWARD THE SKY

Smoke puffs,
spun sugar,
wisps of angel hair,
tufts of cotton,
bowls of popcorn,
a curly lamb
and a polar bear.

White sky-mountains
suspended in aqua,
a sunshade for the pueblo,
all purple and pink
with the setting sun,
pregnant-fat
and rainy-day grey.

New Mexico will make
a cloud-watcher out of you.

Published in *Night Roses*

POISED ON THE BRASS POLE OF LIFE

Carousel pony, bolted in pose,
suspended in permanent prance,
an up and down humdrum life,
a constant boomerang trip.

Pastel pony, painted smile,
do you dream of unshackled runs
in carpet-grass meadows?
Of nuzzling a fantasy-mate?

In a merry-go-round prison,
dizzy with children's giggles,
drowning in calliope sounds,
poised on the brass pole of life,
Just like me!

Shall we jump down
and gallup away?

Published in *Thirteen Poetry Magazine*

THE BALLOON FIESTA

Even before the sun wakes up and peeks
around the Sandia mountains,
balloonists arrive to spread
packs of nylon over the ground
like buckets of paint turned over.
The liquid spots take shape
as fans fill them with early morning air.
Propane burners breathe heat
into the balloons — they sit upright,
resuscitated.
Silently the tinted bulbs
rise from the artists palette.
We are surrounded by colors,
in the middle of an Easter basket.

SEASONABLE

The May-Day girl
flounces her basket,
sprinkles the desert
with a rainbow of petals.

A Summer sun-face,
with puffed up cheeks,
exhales a fire-breath,
glazes the earth.

Autumn's giant hand
flings a flood
of mustard
across the valley.

A Winter goose-cloud
shivers and bursts.
Furry down
blankets the mountains.

WINTER DAY

Snowflakes —
soft as a first kiss,
silent as the blush

Published in *Poets at Work*   Published in *Parnassus*   Published in *Night Roses*

UNDER THE COMFORTER

Outside my frosted beer-mug window,
the weathervane rooster
heads off winter winds.
Warm guilty me
snuggled by the fireplace.

AFTER THE STORM

At the edge of the ski slope
clustered frozen pines,
winter-still, holding their breath,
biding time 'til spring thaw.

HAPPY BIRTHDAY

You're eighty – You old coot.
It's time to celeboot.
At this fancy restauroot
We'll have a hoot!
Lots of red woot,
An expensive rare stoot
And chocolate for desoot.

Oh, we'll live high on the hogoot!
We'll discus all the koots,
Gossip about our palpoots,
Complain of the ailmoots
And cry for past youth mishoots.

Well, my old galoot,
So many years we've been in cahoots,
To you I give a salute
and a hearty toot.
Eighty is not moot,
It's a big pursuit
That none can refute.
So stand on your only boot
You deserve a huge root!

For GG - The Rhymer

THE END OF THE ROAD — NOT EVEN A STOP SIGN

ALL THE ROSES TURNED PALE

Sun fell from the sky that day,
never to be felt again.
Night came with no moon or stars,
Oh, the air was heavy and dreary,
like someone had stifled the world
with a thick blanket.
I laid down to sleep away breath,
and my body made a dent in the earth
from the weight of my sorrow.

He died and took my life,
gone are music and laughter,
the cricket's chirping-song,
and the mating-call of mockingbirds.
Shimmering aspen leaves stopped still,
all the roses turned pale.
I covered my shoulders with his sweater
and his scent brought back his smile,
only to leave me more alone.

Published in the novel *Saving Snowflakes in My Pocket*

THE CYCLE OF LIFE

I have listened to the lonely wind
as he whispered to me through tall pines,
and have known a warming reflection
of the sun's glow, encircling my shoulders
like comforting arms of a friend.
I plucked each petal of the dewy-soft pink rose,
dismantling her like a dancer in seven veils,
searching for her mystery.
One day I cupped a baby bird in my hands,
felt his tiny heart beat with fear
as I placed him back in his twig-home.
I have cried the unbearable joy —
my newborn asleep on my breast,
our hearts intertwined, locked into
impenetrable force of Mother/Daughter.

The end of my time may bring some sadness,
as in the passing of summer,
but be renewed when gentle snowflakes
touch your cheek, refreshing your mind
to continue your own journey.
Let my ashes float free so some small speck of me
may join soil in the valley
and accompany apple blossoms into fruit,
or perhaps nourish a field of sweet strawberries —
my memorial, to soothe your sorrow.
In remembrance of me lift your face to the breeze
and let it ruffle your hair.
Watch young birds, challenged by bravery,
take flight, and learn from their courage.

→

Inhale the scent of fresh velvety roses
and close your eyes, so the memory
of them, and me, will linger in your soul.

As my ashes scatter,
think of laughter we shared
and know you overflowed my heart with joy,
like snow thaw fills the mountain creek
to sate the thirst of new fawns.
All life must end
as even luminescent green hummingbirds,
who delight us with their return in Spring,
one May fail to show up.
As sure as one life ends, another begins,
and someday your Spirit will join mine.
Together we will watch your children's children,
choosing their own path,
continuing their own cycle.

From the novel *The Strawberry Field*

FRIEND OR ENEMY

To the voodoo-image body full of needles,
red-raw elbows, back all bedsores,
pleading, no more shots, no more pills —
Death is a welcome friend,
a Sunday stroll through shady woods,
afternoon tea and whispered secrets,
sitting quietly on the edge of a pine ridge
to watch the deer nibble grass.

To another body, bulging with firm muscles,
running for out-of-reach tennis shots,
diving into sand to lob the volleyball —
Death is a hooded visit
from a stranger swinging an axe,
the lightning strike of despair,
a razor-strop whipping in the toolshed,
the stormy tumbling down into dark.

To loved ones of the lifeless —
it is bitter toxin,
a chunk in the throat.
Death is hard to swallow.

Published in *Black Buzzard Review*

THE VISITOR

Here comes death.
No loud banging
or bragging, no
singing or laughing,
just a light tapping
at my door.
I don't mind his
presence, so quiet.
He brings a gift of calm,
a soothing ease
of body balm.

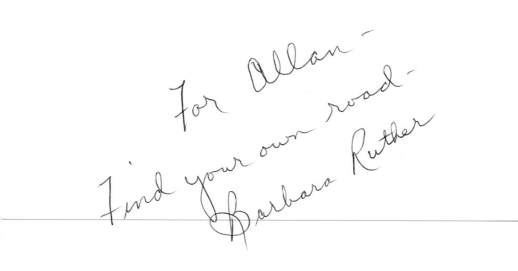

For Allan —

Find your own road —

Barbara Ruther